From the Heart

· POEMS AND MEDITATIONS ·

KIAS EMMANUEL CREECH

BALBOA.
PRESS

A DIVISION OF HAY HOUSE

Balboa Press books may be ordered through booksellers or by contacting:

Balboa Press
A Division of Hay House
1663 Liberty Drive
Bloomington, IN 47403
www.balboapress.com
1-(877) 407-4847

Because of the dynamic nature of the Internet, any web addresses or links contained in this book may have changed since publication and may no longer be valid. The views expressed in this work are solely those of the author and do not necessarily reflect the views of the publisher, and the publisher hereby disclaims any responsibility for them.

The author of this book does not dispense medical advice or prescribe the use of any technique as a form of treatment for physical, emotional, or medical problems without the advice of a physician, either directly or indirectly. The intent of the author is only to offer information of a general nature to help you in your quest for emotional and spiritual well-being. In the event you use any of the information in this book for yourself, which is your constitutional right, the author and the publisher assume no responsibility for your actions.

Any people depicted in stock imagery provided by Thinkstock are models, and such images are being used for illustrative purposes only.
Certain stock imagery © Thinkstock.

ISBN: 978-1-4525-3554-8 (sc)
ISBN: 978-1-4525-3556-2 (hc)
ISBN: 978-1-4525-3555-5 (e)

Library of Congress Control Number: 2011909519

Printed in the United States of America

Balboa Press rev. date: 06/07/2011

dedicated to my siblings,
my parents,
Patricia Reed & Justin Daniels
and also to
Mrs. Ruth Allen Hamilton,
Mrs. Iris Young & Mrs. Nancy Mullins.

Special thanks to Patricia, my sister, my soul twin & best friend. Thank you for giving me hope when it felt like there was none. You changed my life & I can never thank you enough. Without you this book would not exist.

And to Justin Daniels, my brother, my best friend. Thank you for encouraging me & having faith in my writing. This book is for you too! Without a friend like you my life would be empty. I can't thank you enough for being the best brother a guy could ask for.

Contents

Composed September 8, 1998 By: Kias

"Uncertainty"

I'm not sure what to say
But I'm certain how I feel
Everything I'm feeling
Is painful & too real
I've tried hard not to show it
I've tried hard not to say
But every time it touches me
There's no words to convey
For anything this powerful
just cannot be spoken
it's as delicate as glass
and yet cannot be broken
chaotic are the thoughts
that run deep in my mind
painful yet so soft
that they wound me every time
I tried to make provisions
I tried to heal the pain
but sorrow flows within me
and, as blood, runs through my veins
I see a piece of coal
but to me a diamond shines
destruction seeks my heart
like a coming sign of times
I really want to love you
but my hearts not quite sure how
my minds too scared to try it
but it's way far too late now
I try to keep my chin up
I try to shield my heart
but it's on the verge of breaking
every time we are apart
Please don't take me wrong
and don't be lead astray

there are only good intentions
in all I do & say
but hurt is repetitious
and grips me every time
it's hard not to believe
that I'll get hurt again this time
I didn't mean to hurt you
cause I know this sounds so cruel
but it's coming from a wounded
lonely, desperate love-sick fool
just dumb enough to try it
just weak enough to fall
just wishing that I knew
if you loved me much at all

Composed January 7, 2003 By: Kias

"In Your Hand"

Starring at your face
as you lie asleep so still
wondering what you're dreaming of
and how your heart must feel

Knowing what my heart feels
and that it beats in time
to a rhythm & a haunting sound
of a song stuck in my mind

A song I've not forgotten
Its' words for me are real
as I hope these words will find your heart
and you'll begin to feel...

...A love I've not forgotten
for each day you make it new
each day growing stronger
is this love I have for you

Like trains, such thoughts race by me
as I watch you sleep so sound
consumed by all your beauty
and in your love I've found

I take you by the hand
and for eternity it seems
while you lay there sleeping
I get lost in MY dreams

Our hands join close together
and though asleep you hold me tight
a total transformation
Of my world is made tonight

3

The love held deep within you
shines forth right through your touch
and I never knew, myself
that I could love someone so much

for there's not 1 thing about you
that I don't love, please understand
for everyday you hold my heart
and love inside your hand

"Jaguar"

....

There's a force that's within me
too bold to deny
It is strength for the weakened
and makes the strong ones cry

It is love to the hurting
A shield to the young
a song still unwritten
And yet to be sung

A hunger undying
A thirst unrelieved
A gift that you're given
And that's made to receive

A light in the darkness
With honor be it spoken
It lives forever
And for you is unbroken

Timeless and youthful
a pleasure to the eye
a word gently spoken
as the wind through the sky

gentle & caring
yet no one can tame it
everyone feels it
but no one can name it

some have forgotten
though for others it seems
it lives forever
if only in dreams

dreams of you
that don't die away
as real at this moment
as they were yesterday

is it enough
or do you deny
this love for you
that never shall die

resting within me
in silence it burns
for your embrace
it eternally yearns

forced into patience
while wrenching in pain
silenced by the thunder
of the call of your name

falling like sand
through the glass of its time
and while falling, is calling
for your love to be mine

this echo in the distance
constant and still
"I have always loved you
And I always will."

"There's No Me"

....

Without you I am nothing
No love in my heart to give
Without you here beside me
I wouldn't want to live

Your love shines all around me
Like the bright & rising sun
And each day when it comes to shine
My heart has just begun

To feel the love you've given
Each & every day
To never see a shadow
With your love to light my way

Without you I am empty
Like cold words I cannot feel
Lost & long forgotten
Like a tombs unbroken seal

Every day you're in my life
Your spirit sets me free
It's unmistakable
Without you, there's no me

Written February 27, 2011 By: Kias

"I Love You More"

You are what I live for
You're every song I sing
The reason I go throughout my day
At night you are my dream

In the morning you're my sunrise
I breathe you everyday
In the evening when the sun has set
You're there to light my way

I could not live without you
I wouldn't want to try
For without your love for me
I know I'd surely die

You are the prayer I whisper
Each night when I lay down
You're the very words I utter
And still you are their sound

When my night has ended
And the sun comes into light
You are what I focus on
My wings when my spirits in flight

I never have to miss you
You're always here with me
My chains have all been broken
For your love has set me free

Written February 15, 2011 By: Kias

"Mirror Mirror"

Mirror, Mirror, on the wall
Counting all my tears that fall
Have you seen my love go by
Who broke my heart & made me cry
Just how far has it gone
Leaving me here to linger on
Is it true, did I hear you say
That love has died & gone away
Another day I cannot take
That last piece of my heart will break
Mirror, Mirror can't you see
What my love has done to me
It's taken all the hope I had
And left me all alone & sad
Mirror mend my broken heart
And give my love just one more start
This timeless search has got to end
So my poor heart can finally mend
Lift me high that I may soar
And come to know my love once more

Standing By

....

Standing by, waiting for a day
When you'll notice me & look my way
I've waited all this time to see
Your loving arms reaching out to me
So far ignored or perhaps unseen
Like a small breeze through a window screen
It's comforting just not so much
As a stronger wind with a stronger touch
A brighter sun on a brighter day
But I see you turn & walk away
Someday you'll see or at least you'll try
To notice my love's been standing by
It's been waiting all this time to see
What it would take for you to love me

"Sharing my days with you"

I don't wanna leave you here
What would my heart ever do?
Nothing could bring my days more joy
Than spending them with you

Only asking for a day or 2
And still I got forever
That's how long you have my heart
Beyond while we're together

What a joy it is to me
To share with you each day.
A picture is worth a 1000 words
But you're more than my heart can say

All I know is when I'm near you
I dread when the time comes to go
I have nothing to ease my heart then
That's full of love I can't show

I can't be in this world without you
IT'd be like the sun hiding its' face
My heart would die in the darkness
Filled with nothing but empty space

You became my hearts finest treasure
When your love melted all of its' ice
With you to spend now & forever
I would gladly pay the price

As long as I'm here I will love you
For that's all that my heart knows to do
Thank you for your love & letting me
Share my time, my days, with you

Inspired by Denise Blevins & Stevie Nicks

Not Until Today

I never knew til now the love I had for you.
I never knew til yesterday that I'd be missing you.

I wont know til tomorrow, though that may never be; Like every other passing day, how much you mean to me.

When I wake up in the morning & go throughout my day; When I lay down at night you're in my heart to stay.

You'll never be forgotten & if you need a reason why; All the love inside of me, for you, can never die.

For all the tears I've shed lately, Still in my heart I knew; I could never love another the way that I love you.

No one will take your place. Though they may try it is vain; They can't replace the love that grows over & over again.

For until now, I never thought I'd know; The time would come along when one of us would go.

And that I'd be left so empty, Crying & asking "How?" That I could ever feel such sorrow, I never knew til now.

I write your name in the snow hoping somehow you will see; The love that I have that comes to you from me.

My love will never die, dear. It's in my heart to stay; I just never thought I couldn't show it. Not until today.

In Memory of Roman & Eva McFerron

Written Feb. 8, 2011 By: Kias

"My Sweet Valentine"

I write your name in the snow
And a heart I trace for you
While dreaming of your kisses
And your eyes of crystal blue

Thinking of your laughter
And your sweet words in my mind
Telling me about a love
I never thought I'd find

A love I only dreamed of
But never thought I'd see
How could someone sweet as you
Love someone like me?

Much better than red roses
Of this much I am sure
The love that comes from you to me
That's innocent and pure

I'd give everything I own
Down to this heart of mine
If you'd be my love forever,
My sweet valentine

"The Star"

....

My mouth has spoken words my mind can't comprehend
Surely your heart has heard them and you will understand
The language may be different but the feeling is the same
Words that softly echo, there's a star which bears your name
When I look into the heavens I see this star so bright
Even when I close my eyes to my mind its in plain sight
It's touched my heart 1000 times & then maybe more
It's my light in the darkness, when I'm lost it is my door....
That leads me back where I should be, where my soul has always known
Back upon the path I walk, where so many years I've grown
And when our time has ended & we're no where to be found
Your beauty like the star will always be around
Sometimes I feel lost & just when I think I'm through
I feel a tug within my heart that's coming straight from you
It assures me that I'm not alone & you are always near
So when I see that star in the sky it outshines all my fear
We're a chain that can't be broken, a bond forever strong
And as long as we're together, how can we go wrong?
You've become this star to me that I see each night
No matter how dark the sky, I will always see your light....
Shining out upon me & reminding me each time
Forever I am yours & you are always mine.
Now I think about it, those words are not so strange
They describe this life of mine that you have rearranged
Giving it more meaning, more love & light each day
When I get that lost feeling your love will light my way
Never, no not ever, will I wonder where you are
For high up in my heaven, you're my bright & shining star.

"I thought of you"

I thought of you today but then again whats new
hardly a day passes by that I don't think of you

at night I see your picture, its somewhere in my mind
but it always comes to surface for my love is not so blind

it sees you oh so clearly each night inside my dreams
but all the wishing in the world wont bring you back to me

you're gone but not forgotten at least you're not tonight
for when I lay my head to rest in my dreams I'll hold you tight

sometimes my arms around you, sometimes I feel your touch
sometimes I wonder if you knew, would it matter much

but then I know you love me, your ways just not the same
you can't respond the way I do each time you call my name

somehow I know you hear me and I know that you still care
I feel it each & every time my heart sends up a prayer

Someday I will hear you & no matter how long it will be
I'll hold on to the breaking heart that rests inside of me

its the only way I have now so forever now & then
My heart craves to hear you say you love me once again

Inspired by "Gold Watch & Chain"

"I will pawn you this heart in my bosom, only say that you love me again."

"My Only Dream"

The long & flowing river
The endless search for the steel
Of a bridge to carry from my heart
The love for you that I feel

My search indeed is endless
That my love would find your heart
Does that bridge serve to unite us
Or instead, keep us apart

To my heart, that bridge unites us
To my mind, its in danger of falling
In my constant dream, I reach for you
As the voice of my soul is calling

I could try to fool my heart
And say my love for you is not there
But there's no denying the obvious
I do & will always care

Time may work against me
But until then I have to try
To tell your heart my love is endless
And, for you, will never die

And that my darkest hours
By a blinding, brilliant beam
Were broken by your shining love
By you
My only dream.

"On Bitter Winds"

On bitter winds I take my flight
Not knowing where to start
Set upon my journey
Trying to find your heart

Climbing higher with each breeze
Thinking all the way
How your love keeps drawing me closer
While keeping me away

Racing thoughts do blind me
Like cold & winter weather
Knowing we must be apart
Though I wish we were together

As I watch the sun set in the sky
Giving way to stars
It's funny how some freedoms
Keep us behind bars

Watching what you say
Being careful what I do
Looking for every possible way
To bring myself to you

For years I've made this journey
And never tiring at all
If I could only get into your heart
But I just can't break the wall

This time there are no secrets
There are no lies to tell
Just billions of "I love you's"
Trying to pierce that shell

Trying to get through to you
Trying with all my might
Yearning for you to reach for me
And together take our flight

A flight into the heavens
Together you & me
Breaking these walls & shells around us
And finally being free

Onward I must journey
Into the clouds so high
Until I ascend to heaven
Where there's only you & I

Wednesday, April 19, 2006

"At the bridge"

....

I've come here seeking peace, contentment & tranquility. But mostly I have come here to call forward my own energies, to reawaken that part of myself that has been sleeping while I have needed it most. I step out into the breeze & slowly make my way through a corridor of trees, walking on a path that although seems long it also seems empowering. I am at peace. I can't come here & not find peace for it was found within myself & I brought that peace here with me. I can hear the sounds of the river but when I look toward the water I see more than just streaming liquid. I see energy like a thin silver sheet that lays above the water & also seems to flow along with the river as its companion. They work together. Its gentle & soothing but has the power to set my mind free. Walking slightly downhill I am getting closer to the bridge where I can look down upon the river that is flowing full of life. My foot touches the edge of the bridge & I can feel an enormous calm come over me. My heart knows that I've come here to release my cares & set my mind free. I am standing at the center of the bridge looking down with my eyes while my mind journeys far back 4 or 5 miles on the river, to meet the flow of energy that is about to collide with the river & make its way to me. My hands are together, palms up. In my hands are a small pile of white petals. The petals are my cares & they are white because I surrender them to the great sense of peace that is about to take their place. The water & the energy have merged 5 miles back & are making their way toward me. Making myself 1 with my surroundings I feel that it is time. As this massive flow of energy gets just feet away from passing under the bridge, I release the petals. I watch them fall. It seems they fall forever but it is only seconds. Just as they are about to hit the water, I feel the surge get intense. The water & energy hit the petals. As if breaking through glass, the energy has shattered my cares & now carries them far away from me. I am free. But what's more, I am empowered. I know that such peace & joy as this, as the petals through the on going path of the river, must be spread. I am obligated now. Care & compassion are great but are also meant to be shared & carried onward just like those petals. Others must be set free of their cares & knowing what it is like to be free I must help them get to this place......

"Under The Bridge
(Part 2 - At The Bridge)"

....

I turn & continue walking across the bridge. Part of the journey may be over but there are more steps to be taken. At the final step on the bridge there are a number of locations, a multitude of things to see. Turning the corner to my right I come to the top of the steps. Slowly walking down the steps I am deciding which is next but the decision is easy. I step onto the concrete walkway & turn right. Only a few feet & I am underneath the spot where I was when last I let go of pressing thoughts, worries & fears. The walkway underneath the bridge is cool & breezy. I smell the fresh cut grass along the edge of the river, I smell the water with its cold and refreshing power as if it is flowing over me. But its only the breeze that makes its way under the bridge that I am being caressed by. At the lefthand side of the walkway, I stand & hold to the rail watching the river, like a snake through tall grass, make its way past me. It feels good to have let go of so much stress when I was standing on the bridge. But that was just the first step. Holding onto the rail with both hands, I close my eyes & listen to the river. The mad rush of water moving swiftly by me seems like it has a chorus of voices. They sing comforting words. Soothing, tranquil messages letting me know that there are guardians to go with those voices & that they are watching out for me. I reach into my pocket & take out a tiny feather. I release it over the water. Its carried madly, swirling around chaotically finding no place to rest. This feather represents my fears. They may be rational or irrational but they are real. They do me no good but I can't deny their presence. I can do nothing but watch the feather wildly roam & work its way to the ground or to the water, where ever it may land. Again I reach into my pocket & pull out a shiny new penny. I toss it into the river & with a single splash it finds a home at the bottom of the water. Sometimes material things get in the way of the things that matter. Love, compassion, humanity. The river symbolizes those things that matter. Nothing can stop love. It continues to move & work its way through our lives. One last time I reach into my pocket. This time I take out a small bottle containing water. The water in this bottle came from this very river. It was taken while I was here on a previous trip. I've gained so much from coming here it only feels right to give something back &

21

to share the joys I took back with me the last time that I came here & left. I know in order to receive I must give. And freely I give of myself & although I expect nothing in return I never leave empty handed. Before another step is taken I have been filled. What I need is within me. I close my eyes one more time & breathe in the scents of the water and the grass & feel the wind. Embarking on a journey. And the 1st step is taken right here under the bridge....

"Gathering Water (Part 3 - At The Bridge)"

....

Moments have passed as I stand next to the river absorbing the experience. I lean against the railing & look to my left. I see the tables lined against a wall of iron posts. People smiling, laughing, enjoying life under their umbrellas while not failing to interact with others around them. The smells of fresh brewed coffee, grilled steaks & other foods almost seem to collide against the scents of the grass & water from the river. After a few moments enjoying the scenery I step forward from the walkway under the bridge & pursue my serene adventure. The sidewalk, separated by the rail fence from the tables, leads seemingly for miles down a sunlit path. The pavement to my left, the river to my right. The trees that line the river are blowing, their leaves brushing against each other making sounds like whispering voices. The sound is bold, like the sound of the river & while there are birds everywhere singing & making their own sounds, nothing seems to be louder than anything else. Its all calm & blends together like an orchestra. I've reached the north bridge. A nice structure but nothing more than to help cars cross the river. Not much scenic value. But there's an advantage to this end. Steps that lead down into the water. I've got 3 small bottles in my pocket that I've brought here to fill with water from the river. Its a tradition with me. The river itself was consecrated long ago. This is a felt & known fact but nothing that is written in books. I step almost into the water as I set my bottles on the concrete steps, lining them up without their lids. Its not just to collect the water but there's an added bonus to being on this end. When I stand in the water & face the first bridge the flow of the river comes toward me, head on, rather than away from me. And so I stand in the river with my eyes closed & open my arms receiving the breeze & the energy of the river as it races toward me. The water is cold but refreshing. More out in the middle is a large rock where I like to sit & let the river pass on either side of me. When I am there I am solid & braced while the river divides & passes me on my left & my right. I feel as if I am in more than one place at a time. There on the step, waiting patiently in the sun are the 3 bottles waiting to be filled. With the lids in 1 pocket I put 2 of the bottles in the other pocket. This is a symbolic gesture for me but one with much meaning. The first bottle is clear & in a shape almost like a violin. This bottle to me represents Divinity, God, willing to give me not just what I want but what I need & all I have to do is accept it. I plunge the bottle into the river watching bubbles rise as it fills. Tightening the lid on the first bottle I then dry it off & put it in my pocket separate from the other 2 bottles. Now I take out the second bottle. It is also clear but long & narrow like a bullet. This bottle represents me. I plunge it into the river & fill it as I did the first. I take it out & hold it to the sun & realize that this bottle is indeed like me & also like a bullet. On the one hand it has the power to give life, love, joy & rejuvenate others who come in contact with it. Its a constructive use of its gifts. On the other hand having the power to destroy & take life. It isn't what we have but how we use it. We can choose to build life or to tear it down. I dry off this bottle & put it in my pocket then take out the last bottle. This one is blue and larger than the other 2. It also has a dropper made into its lid. This bottle represents my loved ones. I pull it down into the river & fill it. I then put the lid on it, pull a few drops out into the dropper & release the contents of the dropper onto my arm. It reminds me that like the ones I love it is real & is a strong part of me. And like the water in the bottle that those few drops came from, it is a unit. A single force working together. I drop the bottle into the river once more to continue filling it then dry it off & put it into my pocket. With the last few moments breathing in the air that's riding in with the river, feeling the soothing flow of the river as it passes by me, I take in the experience before I walk out of the river & sit on the steps. I appreciate what I have. But I also appreciate what I have to share with my surroundings. This experience is a joint effort with me & nature. As is life....

"Gift To The River (Part 4 - At The Bridge)"

I sit on the steps for a while longer & soak up the warm rays of the sun. Its a beautiful day. I prepare myself for the next steps of this journey. As I sit on the step just above the water, I wade in my own thoughts & realize it is time to move on. I walk up the steps and turn the corner to my right. Placing my hand on the rail of the bridge I look up one last time before going forward to the next location. I feel the warmth of the sun on my face. On across the bridge I walk for only a few feet & step down to my right. I've come to the other side of the river. Standing at the edge of the high walls of the castle I walk along the path between the castle & the river. All the while I have been thinking back on the various locations I had just come from. Thinking of the energy that I have brought from those spots & the great feeling of being at peace within myself. I come to a spot behind the castle, at the edge of the river that sits between the 2 bridges. A spot covered in trees, walkways that end just at the waters edge, leaves of many colors spread out on the ground like veil. I find a place to sit & for what I believe is a place to sit & reflect. But still my journey is not complete yet. I've not left empty-handed from any spot that I've visited. But what have I brought? What have I really offered of myself? I already know that if these questions are in my mind then I haven't given enough. I haven't shown a real appreciation for the lessons I have learned. There are gifts to be received from these locations. Lessons to be learned, sights to behold, peace to acquire. But like the river, the trees, the wind & even the sun. I have my own energy. A part of myself that is inside me that I use to help others. I've been given gifts of energy by my surroundings on this walk. As I sit at the edge of the river, at the end of the walkway, it is clear to me now. I have gifts to give of my own back to those who have brought so much to me. Life is about sharing, about loving & reaching out to your surroundings. Not just to take what they have to give but to give what you have for them to take. Again I step down into the water. With a wall of trees on both sides. I let my thoughts be filled with nothing but goodness, love, beauty, compassion, healing, sincerity. Here I have come to let my own light shine. I make my way over to another rock in the center of the river & sit down. Enough room here to lay back & relax. So I do. My legs stretched out, feet in the water. My arms stretched out wide, hands in the water. I close my eyes & let those warm thoughts flow as a river of energy that springs forth from within me. I give to my surroundings as my surroundings have given to me. Again making myself 1 with them. I feel a cooling surge from the river drawing into me while a warmth extends from me into the river. Its a feeling of compassion. Of 2 who do for each other. A kind & loving relationship between God & man. Between myself & nature. This is what I live for as it lives for me. And our life is eternal....

"On The Balcony (Part 5 - At The Bridge)"

Opening my eyes I find myself completely at peace. Not only do I see my surroundings having my eyes opened but having my inner eyes opened I see what good comes from surrendering to life and letting go of the things that bring me down. Why cling to such things when I can cling to life & breathe more than just the scents of the grass but breathe in contentment & make it a part of my soul. I raise myself from the rock & walk back through the water to the walkway. I can't help but look all around me & take in the day. I continue on, walking toward the right of the castle. I climb the stairs, walk through the corridor & make my way back to my room. Inside, I walk to the balcony doors & push back the curtains to let in the light that is left of this day. I open the door & silence turns to the sound of the rushing river while the cool wind moves through the doorway & surrounds me. I walk over & make a pot of coffee. After its done I pour myself a cup & walk out on the balcony. With a little music playing I sit for a while & watch the river, the wind blowing in the trees, squirrels jumping from branch to branch & although sitting still I am going over the day in my mind. The birds are singing as if they hear the music & are enjoying it as much as I am. Everything feels peaceful, balanced. There are a few friends I wish could come here. I wish they could take this walk & open themselves up to the surroundings. Wish they could let go of the stress & the worry. I wish they could experience life from the inside the way I have here this day. And yet somehow I feel like they have. I feel like I have taken them with me all throughout this day. Then, I have taken them everywhere I've went throughout my life. I will take them with me in my heart when this part of life is over. Until then they are all here with me in my heart. Right here on this balcony.

"The Day"

....

Where is the day that I wait for? The one that shall take me away. The one that shall end in my passing. The one that wont force me to stay. Where is the day that I dream of? The one 'til which one doesn't pass. That I anxiously sit & hope for. The one that shall free me at last. Where is the moon in its rising, which casts rays of light in dark places? The light that brings peace to the darkness & sheds light upon sorrowful faces. To let us know it is watching & tells us to patiently wait. Until the day that we hope for. When it lights our path to a gate. A gate that will lead us so safely to a place where the sun never sets. A place where no harsh words are spoken & arriving there leaves no regrets. Its a place that is home to the spirit. So many are homesick to go. The day that we wait for is coming when we'll rise from this valley so low.

"Egyptian Prince"

....

I'm thinking of a place my eyes haven't seen, but my mind never leaves it not even in dreams. Pyramids, the temples, the people long past. These things are all vivid & their spell still is cast. For years now I've worn its symbols & signs. My Ankh I hold sacred & never leave it behind. I dream of the Pharaohs. I dream of the Nile. And sometimes I see myself dressed in its style. I take part in the rites & with its gods I commune. It keeps my mind focused & my heart in fine tune. Upon my right shoulder I bare the right Eye. With the Ankh on my left one, my heart's in the sky. High in the heavens as signs I await. Reunion with my people I anticipate. Though time stands between us now, in my heart I know. I was there with my people in that land long ago. For a brother I had in THIS time I have met. That its taken so long is my only regret. I call him a prince for he's just that to me. There's royal compassion in his face I see. His eyes are dark yet within them is light. His silence speaks volumes. He could light up the night. His home is in Egypt but his heart reaches out. With a smile he can clear out your fears & your doubt. Just like the land that he lives in endures. His heart seems that timeless & so very pure. Perhaps he's my brother or at least once back then. But today I am grateful just to call him my friend.

"My Circle"

....

Earth below, sky above, let my circle be cast in love. Let it bring comfort, let it hold power. Let my energy live its fullest this hour. Let healing reach out & touch those in need. Let love reach inside them & plant its great seed. Let them know gladness till their hearts overflow. Above all, show them truth & the lies overthrow. Let the elements work with me & the Pantheon take part. To strengthen the weakened & mend broken hearts. May intentions be wholesome & all deeds done be pure. Let love abide & truth endure. Let kind words be spoken & harm kept away. Let the work that I do enhance someone's day. To lift up their heart & set their soul free. So they can be nothing less than the best they can be. May they reach out in a chain reaction. Doing toward others deeds filled with compassion. Spirit Divine, this is my plea. Let my work be pleasing. For such, it must be.

"Into The Light"

....

I'm told my words were harsh but they couldn't ignore the meaning. This abandoned shack of a heart of mine was in dire need of cleaning. I had to mend the wounds. I had to stop the bleeding. I had to heal the hurting. It was starved & due its feeding. A bite or 2 of nourishment to fill the empty space. Another heart with feeling to melt the ice from this place. Ice brought in from cold winds that carried words so hollow. Meaningless expressions that my heart still tried to follow. But silence brought the truth out & the light would cause its finding. Still was hard to see it. So bright it was blinding. Soon it was easy, the truth caused it to break. And that's a sure fire way to tell the real from the fake. Once you distinguish, you know what to do. Its out with the old & in with the new. Some roads are smooth & others are rough. Some journeys easy & some pretty tough. This road & its journey was a hard one to travel. My soul has been broken & my hearts come unraveled. I'm working on that. Its still in the making. But thats no guarantee my heart wont be breaking. But at least this ones over with a hard lesson learned. The bridge was hard to cross but now that I have...its burned.

"My Gift from God"

....

Dear God I love the gift. I accept I just don't understand. Im grateful but do I deserve what you've placed in my hands? I know you must think so or else you wouldn't have sent it. Nor would you have sent it if you hadn't meant it. I find it very beautiful. Its so nice it takes my breath. I'll cherish it forever. Beyond the day of my death. I knew you made beautiful things but WOW what a job you've done. Your craftsmanship is unchallenged. And you've only just begun. Each day it only gets better. More vivid, more sweet & more bright. It leaves me at peace inside & brings light to my loneliest night. Its like a walk next to the water with the comfort of the breeze. No matter what's against me, it puts my mind at ease. So I apologize for questioning. I should know YOU know what's best. And with this gift you've given me I'm nothing less than blessed.

"Plague Of The 1st Born"

It began long ago, atop desert sands; And would strike the 1st born of the red & black lands.

A curse that was placed millennia before; would make its way through our modern days' door.

Born out of truth for the kingdoms to see; there was but 1 God & none before He.

Quite certain beneath Him but none are above; His signs are the rainbow, the cross & the dove.

Back in that time, the initial display; That would spark a stream of magick array...

The staff of Aaron, thrown to the feet; Would change to a serpent by the words he would speak.

The Pharaoh, unfazed, would call for his crew; The same with their staffs THEY each would do.

Later would come the worst fate of all; To the people of Egypt, it would strike them all.

The 1st born child to all of man; Would suffer a plague that would sweep through the land.

Bloodlines were threatened, Kingdoms were shaken; At the thought of their heirs lives being taken.

The plague was removed, the point had been made; And the memories of this horror would fade.

II

Of the place that I told I once was a part; A being with a different heart.

A subject of a different kind; With a weak body but a strong, strong mind.

When I came to pass something occurred; My soul divided, my vision was blurred.

The wheel of time would once more allow; Reentry into this time, now.

But a problem arose when I came to pass through; The 1 that I was would come back as 2.

III

The mission - to find each other again; To rejoin & to the heavens ascend.

We've met, just as was meant to be done; And the spiritual journey has finally begun.

IV

My sister, the other 1/2 of me; Has a gift as I, mystical, you see.

We feel, think & speak with each other; No matter what distance each is from the other.

Each is 1/2 of the others' mind; Its a powerful result when we combine.

Little is left outside of our reach; Ours is something one cannot teach.

It is born within & can't be extinguished; It is fixed in place & can't be relinquished.

Many tasks have been put before us; If weak, it's our bond that restores us.

V

My sister...reversed & rebore; What almost completely destroyed us before.

Back to our time, in attempt to get even; I do not question her intention or reason.

She turned back around & sent on its way; The plague of the 1st born to our time today.

To 1 that has hurt her, time & again; Her bloodline shall suffer what we did back then.

To sum it up, these thoughts I invoke; Of my sisters...just as she spoke.

It refers to the tempers of hornets & bees; There's no harm FROM them if there's no harm to these.

But if you endanger them, its their intent to kill; So if you strike them - kill them,
Or else
you
they
will!

"I'll Love You Always"

I stood at the gate in the light of the moon;
Hoping I'd see you & that it would be soon.
Wishing on stars, sending prayers to the sky;
Waiting for answers as time passed me by.
My heart was so heavy, my spirit so low;
I aimlessly wondered, would you even know.
Could you feel my sorrow? It's all I can do.
To carry this burden of life without you.
I greeted the sun but no light could I see;
The coolness of morning could not comfort me.
The sun caused a shadow & there on the ground;
My poor lonesome shadow was all that I found.
Its been forever since you went away;
My time to be with you is coming some day.
One day for the last time that ole sun will rise;
And cast light upon my tear stained eyes.
Closed tightly in sorrow, closed tightly in pain;
From the last prayer I prayed to be with you again.
My poor heart in sorrow with no love to be shown;
You rest in peace but now I lay alone.
I'll love you always, I shall remain true;
My heart never shall cease to love you.
My love, please believe me. Beyond life's sea;
In that life beyond death, together we'll be.

Composed July 19, 2005 By: Kias

"The Scorpion's Sting"

(Plague Of The 1st Born P II)

A blow was struck just as predicted;
A scar lingers from a wound inflicted.

Memories...of times that have passed;
Have reawakened & are here, at last.

Warnings issued on deaf ears had come;
You ignored the shield & chose to run.

To keep you free & out of harms way;
Yet you silenced the things that I had to say.

Over & over, time & again;
You deceived me then turned & ran.

You looked after me & these actions I savored; But you refused to allow me to return the favor.

Only trying to take care of & love you;
And never trying to rise above you...

Hoping & trying that someday I would be; As much to you as you are to me.

I tried so hard & for so very long;
But your words & your actions confirmed I was wrong.

Where'd I go wrong, How did I fail?
You sank a ship I tried hard to sail.

Kept in the dark & silenced through time; This mountain grew higher & harder to climb.

Then when I thought I was a 1st to know; I was corrected by someone that I barely know.

It seems that something I would learn later on; I was blind to & he knew all along.

You broke the reeds, the pact, the rule;
And made me feel like the worlds biggest fool.

This wound is not healing, the pain grows each day; I'm left with low faith in things that you say.

Though you bestowed upon me an honor, a task; The bright eyes you looked in belonged to a mask.

For over & over I looked passed & forgave; But now it is MY heart that I'm trying to save.

My bitterness grows & may get out of hand; As I remember hard times that passed through our land.

I refuse your offer but I do not ignore it;
For something that died I hereby restore it.

I breathe through it life & such shall it seek; And shall answer only to the words that I speak.

This bee that you struck at, my friend, did not die; It is slightly harmed with revenge in its eye.

Yes, I act out of hurt from pain you inflicted; But a blow of my own was also predicted.

In the name of Ramses from whom you did take; I return the favor. Make no mistake.

The hail was 1 thing, the river another;
Remember that Moses was raised as his brother.

Through the land & the Nile & all places between; I shall show YOU signs that you've never seen.

It could have ended with my flocks & my river; Now I give you a gift that shall cause you to shiver.

He who was destined to inherit my throne; You chose to kill & could've left him alone.

Its been a while. I've not heard from you since; But I hear it is you now who has fathered a prince.

Needless to say of this fact I remind you; What you sent around now comes back to find you.

Death is too easy. Its common yet strange; So a certain structure I instead rearrange.

What was thought to be yours now belongs to another; How's that for revenge, O Moses, my brother?

So pollute my water & smite my land;
But see that which in defense now comes from MY hand.

We had a pact, an agreement, a rule;
Which you broke & in the process made me look like a fool.

So I return your favor, your act & your deed; As I water what you believe is your seed.

The truth shall surprise you though I doubt it will please you; See, you should never bite the hand that feeds you.

So from every Pharaoh who has been on the throne; The wish that you reap from the seed you have sown.

"Broken Chain"

A link in our chain has been broken
No love in your hearts left for me
Brought on by cold words that were spoken
No light at the end can I see
My heart had all the love for you
But you turned & just would not take it
After all this time I adore you
All you want for my heart is to break it
In your shadow through this valley still walking
And in darkness I stumble & fall
In its sadness my heart is still talking
But its words you don't care for at all
Seeing no way, no never
That you'd come to love me again
Knowing we wont be together
My heart seeks only an end
Without you I just cannot stay here
My love for you just will not cease
If you can for me just say a prayer dear
That my broken hearts resting in peace

1:03 PM

"For You, My Friend"

One day in a garden called Eden
The Creator in all of His glories
Was all alone by the waters
No one to tell of His stories.
He fashioned a man in His likeness
With a companion his lifetime to spend;
And found He no longer was lonely
For He had created 2 friends.
Many long years have since passed
He continues to make things today;
All sorts of wonderful friends
He has gathered along the way.
His example He gave me to follow
His loving & kind word was spoken;
Creating wonderful friendships
A circle thats not to be broken.
It was along this pathway I found you
What a wonderful day it became;
My friend, to this day you I cherish.
I smile at the thought of your name.
Each morning I wake I'm reminded,
Each night when I lay down to rest;
Through the day I'm still thinking of you
No doubt that I've been richly blessed.
Of all the Creator has fashioned,
My love forever He's due;
For not one thing could I ask for
That I ever would love more than you.

9:25 AM

"On Wings As A Falcon"

My heart you have captured. Of you my thoughts are filled.
My spirit in you rejoices. My love like a fountain is spilled.
In a constant overflowing for its source cannot run dry.
It doesn't have a limit. For you it exceeds the sky.
And still it keeps on going. It never sees an end.
It only sees the beauty thats inside of you my friend.
That's its' inspiration. Its' courage to keep on going.
Fueling the fire of my love & keeps it forever growing.
You're not just the wind but the wings that keep it sailing.
On wings as a falcon, comes my love to you unfailing.

"Say You Love Me"

You only had to say it,
I only had to know;
You didn't have to mean it
But somehow it had to show.

I only had to hear it,
Yet deep inside of me;
My love for you was bright enough
That every eye could see.

And still my heart kept calling
Though you didn't hear the call;
Asking just 1 question,
"Do you love me at all?"

My mind was always on you
And a day would never pass;
When this dream was long behind me
And I'd be over you at last.

I looked & could not find you,
I waited just to see;
That in our separation
You were missing me.

For I'd been thinking of you
Wishing you were near;
Thoughts that I might lose you
Were all my greatest fears.

For if such love were fatal
Death was approaching fast;
I needed you here beside me
Or else I could not last.

I only wanted you to love me
Thinking, "Soon you will."
Maybe then you'd understand
The love for you that I feel.

But if that never happened
I didn't know what I'd do;
I would never love again
The way that I love you.

Though on deaf ears I'd been calling
My blinded eyes couldn't see;
That what I felt for you
You would never feel for me.

And you never had to mean it
But never talking above me;
For me, to have made it worth it,
You only had to SAY you loved me.

"Roses Are Read"

....

Roses are read, violets are heard;
Sometimes they speak without saying a word.

Just like the roses & the violets as well;
The human heart has secrets to tell.

Dreams that die without being spoken;
Promises made to never be broken.

Visions of love that never shall die;
But here they're just visions so why even try.

You do not love me & yet you insist;
That I am foremost & 1st on your list.

And still from my heart I continue to give;
The love that I have, the life that I live.

To hear you laugh, to see you smile;
For you I walk the extra mile.

But you do not notice, your eyes look away;
And you fail to hear what my heart has to say.

The roses ignored, the violets unheard;
You act as if what they say is absurd.

Soon you'll acknowledge, 1 day you shall see;
That the violets & roses are a lot like me.

Wishing you'd love me, if only you'd try;
For even roses & violets must die.

But unlike the roses & violets can do;
Here & then after, I still will love you.

"My Love"

....

My love is here for you always
Growing stronger with each passing day
Holding you close deep inside me
With no chance of it fading away

It only grows brighter & stronger
A smile to my heart you bring
A smile that is new every second
And a song I am happy to sing

With words that all hearts wait to utter
But a language forever I'll know
You speak it with tokens of affection
You're the water that makes my love grow

For you I'm eternally grateful
More than words ever could say
But with these words I assure you
I'll love you more each passing day

"Always"
....

You, my love, I did not choose
But with you I could never lose
The greatest gift that I've been graced
Was to ever see your precious face
For every time I look at you
I feel there's nothing I can't do
You open my eyes that I may see
That I'm blessed to have you here with me
Everyday you're on my mind
The thoughts are warm & good & kind
If I lost you, my world would die
Bringing pain so deep I could not cry
You cause my heart to rejoice & sing
For to me you are everything
In my dreams you're always there
Letting me know how much you care
With a smile each day I now can rise
And a fresh breath with a sparkle in my eyes
I cherish you & hope that you see
I'm nothing without you here with me
Together forever our souls abide
No matter what distance, we're side by side
For YOU ARE that sparkle in my eye
And my love for you will never die
So take this promise, for its pure & true
Eternally & always......I love you.

"In That Instant"

Like a full Autumn moon that brightly glows
Whatever I do, my love for you shows
Bright enough that all eyes can see
Your love has made a change in me
Had no idea what your love could do
In an instant I became someone new
Someone life gave a second chance
And filled that life with love & romance
Constantly my mind is graced
With an image of your precious face
In my mind your name is repeating
My mind is still while my heart is beating
As if there's a message it waits to convey
Of a love that strengthens each passing day
Every day it grows more intense
I've never been the same person since
But who I am now I'm happy to be
And I owe it all to your love for me.

"Empty House"

....

The old home place was abandoned
When momma & daddy had past
They left for a mansion in heaven
To abide with the savior at last

Daddy left home late one summer
Leaving our family behind
Just me, my momma & brother
And our saddened hearts & minds

Our hearts were starting to mend
Though the loss was a hard one to swallow
But worse would come for us boys
When in a year our momma would follow

For months she would stand in the window
In the sun or the pouring rain
Whisp'ring the name of our father
But he would not be home again

Inside her heart was dying
For the one she truly loved
Was no longer by her side
But was waiting in heaven above

One night as she lay in bed
Her arms stretched to the sky
She whispered daddy's name again
As a tear fell from her eye

A smile across her face appeared
For the first time in a year
As she closed her eyes in death
And faced it without fear

At the old abandoned home place,
I sometimes sit & stare
But thru the window, no one's watching.
Just emptiness is there.

"Blue Rose"

....

A rose among many with a heart that is true
But my blood red color has now become blue
My petals are dying & they fall all around
Blown by the wind & cannot be found
My spirit is fading, my color is pale
And my storm beaten body is beginning to fail
What I will become I don't really know
I no longer care, I'm ready to go
I serve no purpose but food for the eye
I bow to the heavens to let me die
My spirits contrite & my poor heart is broken
Haunted by words that never were spoken
Yearning for love I never could find
Seeking a heart & compassionate mind
But love is not blind, I clearly now see
I was born to a world with no place for me
Just a freak of nature, a sore to the eye
An eagle that will never fly
A lion that can never roam
There's no place here I can call home
From where ever I came I must go back
Before this pale blue rose turns black
Oh home away & high above
Let it be me you're thinking of
Your arms of love, summon me to
Cast love upon your rose so blue
Let me wake unto eternal dawn
I beg you, bid this rose be gone.

"Going Home"

All is calm but not so bright
As I gaze into the stars tonight
Looking for an entrance clear
To my home so far away from here
That an angel would come down to me
To take me away & set me free
To shield me with protective wings
From this world, this life & other things
That the journey finally & soon would start
And relieve the pain of my heavy heart
That my soul could rest & no longer roam
But be at peace cause its going home
This wish on the northern star so bright,
Let my journey home begin tonight.

"With Joined Hands"

Nothing shall distract me
My eyes are on the prize
I eagerly await the day
I look into your eyes

The day we both are seeking
Most others seem to dread
But with great anticipation
We await this day instead

We see it as a journey
That only will begin
When we step into forever
And our mortal lives shall end

Eternally I am grateful
As the seas are to the sands
As we head toward safe haven
With our joined hearts & joined hands

"Forsaken"

A wildwood flower lies beneath a willow;
The earth for my blanket, a stone for my pillow.

Consumed by sorrow, my love does not know;
I bowed to defeat & I no longer grow.

You had forsaken, to another you fled;
This forgotten wildflower, storm-beaten, is dead.

I fell to neglect on that cold, lonely day;
When the only one that I loved went away.

You were the only love of my heart;
You loved another & it tore me apart.

With a sad, lonely heart I fell to my knee;
I looked to the heavens with this tearful plea.

"For one last time please lay me down;
To rest in peace beneath the ground.

That one that I love, my heart did forsake;
My heart fills with sorrow & soon it shall break.

The pain is too great & grows stronger each hour;
Have mercy upon your wildwood flower."

An icy hand took hold of me;
And now I lay beneath this tree.

Caused by love that you left unspoken;
My forsaken heart now lies here broken.

"Walk Into the Light"

....

She walks the long narrow path with trees arching over her high above. A long white gown covers her as if she is making her way through her house to go to bed. She stands at the edge of the covered walkway & lets the breeze blow by her face. It blows her gown making it stand out like a hoop is holding it out. Looking like a tiny ballerina inside of a music box. Her eyes closed in thought, she stands there in complete comfort. She collects herself; her thoughts, her dreams, her spirituality. She stands beneath the trees that seem to bow over her in protection. They shade her but the shadows they cast are not an evil darkness but rather a reminder that the light is just ahead. She sees the light too! It shines down like a pillar in the center of the forest. She awaits the moment she is standing in it. Its her ritual. It has great meaning to her. It follows the path of her life. Once in hopelessness, darkness & shadows but deep inside her she always knew that only one thing caused a shadow. A light! And that light was just ahead of her. It waited for her just like she waited for it. But she had to realize that she needed it. She had to know that she was going to have to make the effort to walk into the light & not stand there in the darkness that only hovered over her like a hungry animal waiting to attack her. The breeze that pushed against her face pushed for a reason. As if it was a set of hands brushing by her face to be placed at the sides of her head & pull to her to come forward. Come, my dear, into the light. Love is the light that awaits to illumine your soul. She stepped out into the center of the forest as part of her routine. The warmth of the sun covered her like a shield. She was reminded of the great life she had been given when she let go of her former self. She is a new woman now. New in the light of love. You see the trees. You see them in your mind. They hover over you like a cloud, a veil. But if you really look you can also see that the light is just ahead of you. Don't be afraid, let it surround you. Walk into the light.

"Red Candle"

Red candle in your tiny holder green
Take me to the place I've never seen
A name I carve into your wax
A date of birth & other facts
This info of the 1 I love
The 1 I'm always thinking of
As I look into your flame so bright
And wish I will, no room for might
Draw the one I seek to me
I am the shore, come here my sea
Let what you feel now multiply
Let the games begin & the magick fly
As my silent bell shall toll
It inside my heart & your soul
Both of which feel quite the same
Burning like this candles flame
Burning with the fire of love
Each other is what we're thinking of
Oh candle with your loving fire
Consider this, my hearts desire
And bring the 1 I love to me
Seal our bond! So it must be!

"Inside My Heart"

I think of you often, whatever I do;
My face bears a smile when I'm thinking of you.
I take you with me where ever I go;
You're part of me & my very soul.
Through the valley or the mountain so high;
I always find you by my side.
I don't have to see you, you're here in my heart;
I'm with you also & will never depart.
I talk with you always, inside my mind;
And feel your love so good & kind.
From the start that love you've shown;
Reminding me I'm not alone.
Each night when I lay to sleep;
I know that you will always keep....
Me inside your loving arms;
And I'm certain I will not be harmed.
As you, your love, to me impart;
I carry you inside my heart.

"Sacred Space"

....

When I'm feeling out of place
I go into my sacred space
There I feel a soothing breeze
That sets my restless mind at ease
I hear the river flowing by
While I'm looking to the sky
And soon my cares have gone away
Like the sun at the end of day
I smell the rain that lingers close
The earth to bless with a healthy dose
A welcomed rain not 1 I dread
To wash me clean & clear my head
Leaving me without a trace
And happy in my sacred space

6:57 PM

"Invoking"

....

Calling on elements & creatures of flight
Come & take part in my personal rite
Come join in & lend me your best
Enhance my magick, illumine my quest
As I walk the Circle requesting your presence
Your participation, your quintessence
Manifest in your chosen hue
And a form that is uniquely you
I begin in center where I take position
To cast my circle in my own tradition
Preparing my soul for a sacred feast
At north point make my way to east
Feeling the air & all that is pure
Feeling confident & very secure
To the south my hearts desire
Is to feel a bright spiritual fire
It does not harm, it does not burn
It fills my being & helps me learn
It rises high to, in silence, express
I now must make my way to west
To waves unseen & yet so high
They disappear into the sky
Drenching like a mystic sea
They magnify my energy
Buried by waves to rise in new birth
Water directs me to northern earth
Sealing this Circle, sealing me in
I summon Divinity that I may begin
Inside my Circle that eyes cannot see
I let my energy emerge from me
In its fullness & brightest light
I give thanks for this sacred night
Which I have chosen to show my love
To my companions here who dwell above

No words I could speak would ever impart
The love for them within my heart
I give thanks for the thorns as well the roses
And this Circle in my heart that never closes

"Bubbles"

....

A new ritual of mine of which I'm fond
Performed with a bottle & a tiny wand
In this I'm sure you will discover
When darkness like a cloud may hover
Like the bond of candle & wick
There's light within this simple trick
This bottle contains a liquid clear
Free from sorrow, pain & fear
I take the bottle in my hand
In the grass or on the sand
Into the wand I blow my troubles
Releasing them in tiny bubbles
I watch my cares all drift away
And smile cause its a beautiful day
For hours these bubbles I stand & blow
And watch all the negativity go
Into the air til without a sound
The bubbles burst & to the ground
My troubles, sadness & the hurt
Crash & sink into the dirt
And then I find a nice surprise
All that stuff can fertilize
The earth until the flowers grow
Then only love & beauty show
For just like paper comes from wood
Bad things can be made to good
So now when you are weighed with troubles
Send them away in tiny bubbles

"Coffee, Candles & Celtic Music"

Sitting here in my little room on a cozy Autumn Sunday afternoon, I can relax & be as carefree as I want to be. I put on a pot of coffee & while it brews I sort through candles of various colors until I find one that fits the occasion & also my mood. I find one orange like a bright pumpkin. It has the scent of spiced cider. I light the candle & turn on some soothing music with a celtic feel to it. Over at the cupboard I have a special cup I drink my coffee from. Styrofoam is too generic & lifeless for such a special occasion. I take out my white cup with a picture of a little village on it. Next to it in the cupboard is a little silver baby spoon I use for a stir stick. I fix a cup of coffee that is so fresh that drops are still falling into the pot from the brew basket. After I add a little cream & sugar, I step over to the tiny couch, set my cup down on the coffee table & walk over to the bar where my bright orange candle is burning with a tall, heart-warming flame. I bring my candle to the coffee table with me as music fills the room. Sharp sounds of Celtic fiddles & stringed instruments paint a picture of peace & tranquility for me & the occasional passer by to relax to. Lying at the edge of the coffee table is a newspaper with story after story to tell. But compared to the stories being illustrated & written in my imagination the newspaper is dull & boring. Out the window I see the sun setting & streetlights popping on like lightning bugs that frantically spark the night sky in wide open fields. The October breezes are cool & comfortable while the coffee, candlelight & music give me a cozy warmth that is more a warmth to my soul than my body. I look with the eyes of my imagination & I can see little sparks of glowing light here in the den with me. Dancing around to the tune of the music. The night is long & dark but not boring at all. There are plenty of things to ignite my senses into the crackling fire that waits to warm my heart. I lean back with cup in hand, breathing in the aroma, bringing the taste of the brew to my lips, listen to the soft music & watch the flame of my candle as it dances & displays the deep sense of peace & tranquility that I can sit here & feel for as long as I wish.

"For Gary & Larry Reed"

This is for 2 of my brothers
My last visits been quite a while
But each time I go up to see them
They give me their love & a smile
Their place is surrounded by fences
And trees that tower above
I get a feeling of peace overwhelming
As well as their brotherly love
The main site there is quite touching
It makes ones tears hard to hide
To see these twin brothers are resting
With a single stone, side by side
They came to this world with each other
Together forever to stay
And when it was time to go home
Together they went their way
Bittersweet in some ways
But sweeter somehow still
The closeness of twin brothers
Is eternal on that hill

"Free (At The Bridge - part 6)"

Gathering only myself & my senses, I realize that a walk back to the bridge is a must for me. Although I am quite a distance from my favorite spot to go & relax, the beauty in it is that it is in my heart, my soul & my mind. Going there is as easy as wanting to. And I more than want to, I have to! I seek the white flower. It isn't a literal flower although one can be used to represent the ideas & intentions I have in my heart to come back to myself. The white flower to me is a symbol of inner peace & tranquility, solitude & comfort. I close my eyes & in the endless worlds of my mind I soar to the city of my hopes & dreams. I make my way to the spot where my body has been but my heart is never away from. With the grace of a butterfly, the speed of a dragonfly & the determination of a falcon I travel miles away to what is only a short distance in my mind. As a quiet whisper I hear the rushing & flowing sounds of the river that captivates my senses everytime I am near it. The sounds get a little louder as I get closer. I have a need to approach the bridge on foot. Its the ritual of the walk, the journey on the gravel path to the grassy edge that meets the end of the bridge. I descend at the arched doorway at the top level of my beloved castle. I stand there at the rail that overlooks the river feeling the wind against my face & smelling the sweet scents of the trees that line each side of the river as well as the river itself. I turn & make my way down the steps & spiral down to the ground level archway. Now I begin the walk toward the bridge. The symbolic journey of working toward inner peace. Just as before I stroll slightly uphill on the blacktop sidewalk underneath trees that stand on each side of me & seem to bow, welcoming me back home. I get to the grass & gravel bed near a bench beneath a tree. The breeze blows by me, pushing me, guiding me onward. I cross to the edge of the sidewalk & as my feet touch the end of the bridge I feel the breeze get stronger as if to confirm that I am at the right place, I am home again. I take a few more steps til I am once again back at my bridge, looking down to see the river flowing forward, underneath me. It does feel like home here. Nothing has to be done really. Its the simple fact that I am here that releases my spirit & my senses from the cell of stress it has been temporarily caged in. But I'm here now & I am free. In the corner of my eye I see a small bird land on the rail of the bridge next to me. It turns its head toward me, makes a bowing gesture & takes off straight through the trees that bow over from each side of the river. It has greeted me & welcomed me back home. Back to myself. Back to inner peace & tranquility. In its own sweet little way it reminded me that as long as I am here I am ok & there is nothing that could ever harm me here. For here I am free.

"Magick White Flower"

I will weave with the mixture of shadow gray air
With the thunderous waving & rain in my hair
And the lightning so bright as it veins through the sky
As the black birds in circles are treats to my eye

I was taught what I needed I'd find deep within
She said not to fear it but make it my friend
And to listen to voices that spoke from inside
To believe that my spirit with storm winds will ride

The ride not in chaos but fully controlled
But I must let my magickal wings unfold
And make sure in my life that God is the center
In Spring, Summer, Autumn & Winter

He gave me magick as a powerful gift
By His wind my wings will lift
His gracious gifts did not then end
He blessed me with my spirits twin

She taught me that our gift was true
Together there's little that we can't do
2 bodies that believe are one spirit
Whenever she speaks I always hear it

No matter the distance we are from each other
She's more than my sister, I'm more than her brother
We're soultwins & this fact we know
Our bond will never cease to grow

We're a unit, now & forever
A chain that cannot break or sever
Although we're 1, I admire her power
My loving twin, my magick white flower

"Hazel"

....

I show my honor on this day
For a lady who has gone away
Not just a lady but a mother dear
Who to my heart is very near
Her twin boys & her daughter too
To my heart are siblings, loyal & true
The boys also are laid to rest
By a bond with them my heart is blessed
Their sister & I share a spirit
When she thinks of me, inside I hear it
An eternal bond with these dear friends
A kind of love that never ends
I hold them close within my heart
And from them I shall never part
To me they mean the world & more
They're my life & what I'm living for
But this day belongs to their mother
I love you, mom. Love, your son & their brother.

"Patricia"

....

No sister could be better
No best friend or a wife
Could match or bring more joy
that what you bring into my life

No twins could be as close
No bond could be as strong
If anyone said otherwise
They couldn't be more wrong

You complete my very existence
Since you came there is no goal
For I'm overwhelmed with happiness
To share with you my soul

You became a source of strength
My guide, my hope, my light
I trust you without question
And thank God for you each night

You're the twin of my spirit
I'm proud to be yours too
My life would mean nothing
If I had to live it without you

But our hearts & souls are one
And I'd want it no other way
Always know that I love you
More than words could ever say

Black Eyes

Current mood: sad
Category: Writing and Poetry

Black eyes dark with sorrow have nothing left to see
Longing for the vision to see you here with me
But that vision is a dream, a tear upon the face
A painting without color, a soul that has no place
A fire ablaze in the distance diminished to a spark
Was all the light that was left but now its growing dark
I see you in the nighttime in many dreams so sweet
I hear echoes that are calling your name that I repeat
This mask that hides my face a river of tears has stained
Sweet memories of your laughter are all that has remained
I pray to hear your voice & wonder if mine is heard
Sweat & tears bleed from me as I utter each little word
My hearts doors are wide open, I beg you, come inside
For ever since you went away a part of me has died
The part that lives to love you forever shall go on
But without your love to surround me no day shall ever dawn
Hear me in your mind, may your heart forever know
The love inside my heart for you has no place else to go
My love for you is endless, I just pray that you will see
Black eyes dark with sorrow in your dreams that belong to me
They wish upon a star shining in your heart so bright
To let me feel your love again & give these dark eyes back their sight.

Our Constant Dream

....

Current mood: anxious
Category: Writing and Poetry

In my mind I'll always see it
The home so strong I crave
Its a yearning deep inside me
Reached only by the grave
It isn't a fear I have
But intense dreams I feel
Of falling on my knees at last
At my home that I know is real
As I hold to the hand of my sister
Who equally is craving
The home we're willing to die for
No intensions of this life saving
Joyous tears shall fall
Brushed away by gentle hands
That shall raise our smiling faces
To behold the sunlit lands
And gently remind & tell us
We're no longer dreaming of
The day we wait to save us
And that shall raise us into love
Those cold nights that we cried
Feeling lost & out of place
No longer shall infest our minds
But be forgotten & erased
I can hear the sound of singing
Of a sweet & peaceful song
And a voice that softly whispers
Don't cry, it wont be long
Just look up to the heavens
And set your eyes upon a star
Just know that I'll be watching

And when you call I wont be far
I understand your hurting
For each time you see it rain
My loving tears are falling
For I hurt when you're in pain
But when the rain is over
And sunlight fills the sky
Its my love reaching out to you
That love your tears shall dry
I know that you are waiting
And I know you hear my song
I love & miss you also
I'll come get you before too long
These thoughts are a constant echo
They help to ease the sorrow
What gets us through today
Is the hope that we'll go tomorrow
Til that day our hearts will see it
In our hearts we always know
Even if its not tomorrow
The day comes when we'll go

The Dream of Home

....

Current mood: accomplished
Category: Writing and Poetry

Another dream began that outside winds could not break
But this dream I was having was while I was awake
Like a movie I was viewing, I watched each vivid scene
My thoughts unmoved throughout the night from this place serene
This time I heard no voices but saw faces passing by
Was a secret in my heart withheld that I could not deny
Obsessive contemplation, waiting for days to pass
A long awaited wish I had that no other could surpass
My friends were all around me in a room lit dim and poor
Huddled with 2 in a corner but there was something I waited for
My visions kept to myself to prevent any interference
I waited for a summoning that sparked a sudden disappearance
I saw us 3 conversing while my mind got a separate call
I felt my breath grow heavy & my pulse rate start to fall
My brother sat beside me talking to a red haired girl
While my mind was elsewhere, a place out of this world
A time beyond all measure, hearing a voice my soul well knew
A message loud & clear received while intense energy grew
The room grew white & hazy, my brothers voice was hallow
I refused to call attention for the news would be hard to swallow
In my mind, my twin was calling, almost desparate yet sublime
With sheer anticipation she was telling me, "It's time"
Like a zombie, dazed & starring, I was too frozen to shudder
My brother saw me motionless but a name he heard me utter
In an instant he was frantic but her spell he could not break
For I was clinging to her energy til my body began to shake
Drawing from my twin I got the energy to rise
I turned toward my brother while tears welled in his eyes
My destiny approached that I craved too much to ignore
I kissed my brother on the cheek & walked toward the door
A car pulled in the driveway, its lights were brightly shining

I walked the path it lit for me, determined, not repining
My twin was in the drivers seat, her eyes almost aglow
With a steady voice she called to me, "Come on, its time to go!"
I got inside the car & with a voice so sharp & clear
I sent a warning to my brother, "Keep yourself right here!"
In a hurried speed we left with pleased & determined minds
I looked back to see lights that were coming close behind
On a road long & dark this journey had progressed
The car behind was my brothers, he ignored the warning I expressed
Our car gained its speed as we tried to flee his sight
To spare him from seeing what was coming tonight
Twice I felt the car slip but she held it in the road
A look of determination was the only thing she showed
Anxiously I was watching, he was still so close behind
I took her by the hand just as bright lights deemed us blind
I felt the car go airborne, seemed like hours going by
As I put my arms around my twin, flames lit up the sky
I felt that I was rising upon a calm & lukewarm breeze
My feeling was confirmed when I looked down seeing trees
I looked around so frantic for my twin I could not find
Then was comforted by her voice saying "We're now 1 soul, 1 mind."
I asked her of my brother. I was told to make it fast
Then as one we stood before him, for the 1st time & the last.
Although he could not see us, he felt our arms embrace him
It was hard seeing him cry knowing it was the last time I'd face him.
With one last flow of energy, we brushed a tear from his eye
We kissed him on the cheek & softly whispered, "please, don't cry."
We told him that we loved him & that things would be ok.
Then in a flash of velvet color, at last we were on our way.

It Must Have Been Love

Current mood: thankful
Category: Writing and Poetry

When I think of when I met you
The thought is never old
The day you came into my life
My blue moon turned to gold
Thoughts of you amaze me
I lose myself in such
Your power sooths my soul
Everytime I feel your touch
I look into your eyes
And am captured by your stare
To see the beauty of your spirit
And the beautiful place that's there
My eyes turn to the heavens
My sincerest thanks I send
For the journey that I walk with you
That's so sweet & never ends
I hold you in my heart
To God your name I speak
For you're the strength I prayed for
When once I was so weak
I'm blessed beyond all measure
I'm moved each night to tears
By your love thats wrapped around me
And shelters me from fears
Such beauty deep within you
Such love I've never known
Such gratitude I have for you
For that love to me that you've shown
You are my gift from heaven
My light from God above

Why He gave me such a precious gift
Guess it must have been love
I'll cherish you forever
In your shadow I'm honored to stand
My heart is overwhelmed each time
I simply take your hand
In your smile I take great comfort
You're in my heart to stay
I can't deny I'm blessed with you
Beyond what words can say
How could I deserve such greatness
What could God have been thinking of,
To have given me such a precious gift?
It must have been love.

"You Are Everything"

If I could do for you what all you've done for me
I would make you happier than anyone could be

I'd fill your life with sunshine & clear away the rain
I'd bring true all your dreams & take away your pain

I'd make sure everyday that passed would see your smiling face
And make any fear you've ever known be totally erased

I'd fill your heart with laughter & fill your soul with gladness
I'd surround you with serenity & keep you free from sadness

Anytime you'd call on me you'd know I'd always hear you
You'd never find yourself alone for you'd always have me near you

I would never cause you pain, I would never cause you sorrow
As much as I would love you today, I'd love you more tomorrow

You've given my life purpose & each day my strength renew
I only wish that everyone could have someone like you

With you there is no sorrow, all pain is hid away
My hope in each tomorrow comes from your love each day

I never feel alone, that thought can't even start
For anytime I need you, you're deep inside my heart

Filling it with laughter & joy beyond all measure
And a richness unmistakable for you are my hearts treasure

I've only had one dream that you have made to live
This life that once was empty is filled with love you give

Which just a simple thought of you, no one can help but see
I have no need for anything. You're everything to me.

"My Voice Will Haunt You"

My dreams are wrapped around you
My visions hold you close
When thoughts of me surround you
You cast them off as ghosts

But deny me all you want to
And say my love's untrue
You can run for the rest of your lifetime
But there's 1 thing you can't do...

Deny me what I'm feeling
For I know what's in my heart
And the years in all their numbers
Will not tear us apart

When I cannot be near you
The wings of my love take flight
And though you say my love is blind
You are always within my sight

Deceitful hands may hide my eyes
But in this truth, be free
That even when I close my eyes
Still, you are all I see

All things that lie before me
All places I may go
Bring me to this final truth
That you & I both know

Though it might be hard to understand
It's a simple fact to see
That the only thing my love desires
Is your love, in return, for me

I know it sounds a lot to ask
Yet all that I have, I'd give
Cause the heart that's in me is dying fast
And requires your love to live

My very soul is aching
And I don't say this to taunt you
But my heart calls out its love for you
And the sound of its voice WILL haunt you.

inspired by the song "Silver Springs" by Stevie Nicks

Composed April 5, 2007 By: Kias

"On Route To Avenge"

....

(Cobra & Vulture)

Back where oasis & desert join hands
Where the cobra & sun move over the sands
Where the vulture rests high on Pharaoh's brow
Come & I shall take you there now
Back to the not so ancient of days
To expose intruders & their criminal ways
In the study of Archeology's name
They robbed Pharaoh's tomb without guilt or shame
They stole his belongings, disturbed his rest
Removed his bindings & took charms off his chest
They ripped fingers from hands to steal his rings
Among other disrespectful things
According to the papers there quest went well
But there were some things the papers didn't tell
Things foretold millennia before
Would begin to manifest that November 4
The year was AD 1922
When an ancient Pharaohs rest would be through
A warning plainly before their eyes
They ignored & so welcomed their own demise
The 1 with audacity to call himself Lord
Was symbolically beheaded by Pharaoh's sword
Carter, the intruder with the least respect
Lived longer so on his comrades deaths could reflect
Warnings were issued but on deaf ears would fall
They acted as if they didn't care at all
Scoffing & calling us superstitious
But 1 myth came to life & proved quite malicious
As the Pharaoh's tomb they were breaking into
A protector of his was going to work too
Right out of the hot & dry desert sand
Was rising a cobra at Ra's command

Once fully manifest it went on route
A consequence to bring about
On a winding path to Carnarvon's home
That was unattended but not exactly alone
Making its way within the walls
To the enticing sounds of a canary's calls
Curling around the base of it's cage
Its' eyes aglow with Pharaoh's rage
Winding upward with the cage door in sight
With a message to deliver that night
It entered with hardly any effort at all
It swallowed the canary & ceased its call
This historical fact is what these words are for
For it'll happen again JUST LIKE before
Now if the gods, such protection to dead kings are giving
Imagine what they'll do for the living
No need for me to ponder such things
I'm cloaked in Isis' protective wings
For I, as the Pharaoh & you, as the invader
Was good to you but you became a traitor
On me, your accusations & judgments were cast
And that was something I could not look past
You called me evil & said I was wrong
Your false accusations to me don't belong
For you I worked for protection & to heal
Your very emotions I could always feel
If just 1 tear were to fall from your eye
It was I who was there to wipe it dry
But it was YOU who turned your back on ME
And now its your blinded eyes that so soon shall see
The protective vulture & cobra, too
Have a message that they are carrying to you
Whether or not you are there to retrieve it
I dare say, its your canary that shall receive it
You can't make it right nor the heart can you bribe
Of this ancient Egyptian magickian & scribe
For just as the Pharaoh, they look after me too
And are well aware of the pain you've put me through
I could've lived with silence, you could've walked away

Instead you wounded me with what you had to say
Remember those who invaded Pharaoh's tomb?
How for their hurtful ways there was no room?
Their disrespect earned no 2nd chances
Like that of you, for whom my cobra dances
He rises from the sands as he did in that day
And to your not so unattended home makes his way
To coil around the base of your cage
It's eyes aglow with this magickians rage
Winding upward with the cage door in sight
To avenge the pain brought on by your fight
While half its body shall hold tight to the beam
Its hood shall open & shatter your dream
With a fully opened hood & fire in its eyes
Fueled by your judgments & vicious lies
To avenge my pain & guard my heart
That you carelessly wounded & almost broke apart
But just like Carnarvon on that canary's fateful morning
It is only fair that you too receive warning
Symbolic as Egypt, here's a warning & hunch
It isn't a canary that shall be my cobra's lunch
At any rate, 1 alone would not do
So there's plenty my cobra has in store for you
Things spread out evenly, not all shall come at once
Just like your words that wounded me, it's the thought that counts
Each & every one of your "canaries" you cherish
My cobra shall come for & they each shall perish
The cage door's been broken & is apart from its hinge
Be watchful! My cobra's on route to avenge

"In Your Arms"

I've had no 1 to love me
the way you always have;
The harbor lights don't shine for me,
It's you who lights my path.

Its you who lifts my spirit
With every smile I see;
With your sounds of laughter
More life you grant to me.

You embrace me with compassion,
With such care you hold my soul;
Every thought inside my mind
Is there for you to know.

Your words you speak so softly
Yet the meaning is so bold;
You combat my every fear
& warm me from the cold.

I'm met with reassurance,
The times are far from few;
That you let me know you love me
While I wonder what I do...

...To make you feel so strong
In the love you have for me;
While I try hard not to lose it
You always give it free.

As if its all you want to do
to show how much I mean;
Just getting to be close to you
Is a feeling so serene.

All light within existence
Compared to you is pale;
All winds are gentle breezes,
Its you who guides my sails.

Without you I am nothing
But am comforted to find;
We're 1 for I am yours
& I know you're always mine.

My hope when none is present,
My peace when I can't see
That all the world may turn its back
But you're always here with me.

For once I feel I matter
Where I never did before;
When I feel I've reached your limit
You show you love me more.

When your arms are put around me
& no more you could be near;
My heart fills with contentment
& I lose my every fear.

My sword to fight the darkness
When weak, my strength to live;
When afraid you are my comfort
& still your love you give.

When I feel alone I hear you
For you are just a thought away;
Then, I'm always thinking of you.
It's what gets me through each day.

For you I'm ever thankful
You're my gift from God, I know;
He must really love me too
For in you, my gift, it shows.

There's not enough that I can say,
What good would mere words be;
To tell you how much I love you
& how much you mean to me.

I realize that you know it,
It never hurts for me to say;
Not only that I love you
But that I love you more each day.

I've never felt so loved
Quite like I have from you;
And I've never had to question
If, in fact, that love is true.

I'd never want you to leave me,
I just wanted you to know
I don't want to leave you either
But if somehow I must go...

There is 1 thing I ask for
And if to this task you could see;
As to where I would spend that final moment
There'd be no better place for me.

Then the place I've always cherished
That gave me so much love;
The only place compared to it
Is the home that waits above.

In this place there'd be no sadness,
No isolation or fear;
All I'd know is pure compassion
From this place I hold so dear.

All I'd know is love
And never again know harm;
If I could spend my final moment
Safe within your arms.

"Rescued"

....

Roses on fire,
Cast down to a blue-white flame;
A love discarded
Without finding as much as a name.

Burned down to ashes
That were carried away by the wind;
Quickly forgotten,
Never to be seen again.

Riding the winds
But finding no place to call home;
Fully aware that
Its' journey could me made alone.

On few occasions,
Thinking a home it had found;
Only to discover, once again,
It had been thrown down.

A face in the shadows
Painted in black, white & gray;
Void of expression
But a heart full of words left to say.

But no one could hear them,
On deaf ears they seemed to fall;
Some day they could be silenced
Never to be spoken at all.

Then picked by a hand that adored it
And that would never let it go;
Meant to be together
As they were so long ago.

At last a hand to hold it,
This rose once thrown to the fire;
Finally knowing what it was like
To be some hearts desire.

A dream it thought had died
Had finally come true;
When this lost & dying heart
At Last, was saved by you.

Notes

Notes

Notes

Notes

Notes

Notes

Notes

Notes

Notes